Child's Guide
to the
Seven Sacraments

BY ELIZABETH FICOCELLI

ILLUSTRATIONS BY ANNE CATHARINE BLAKE

Paulist Press
New York/Mahwah, N.J.

Caseside design by Sharyn Banks
Caseside illustration by Anne Catharine Blake

Text Copyright © 2005 by Elizabeth Ficocelli

Illustrations Copyright © 2005 by Anne Catharine Blake

Library of Congress Cataloging-in-Publication Data

Ficocelli, Elizabeth.
    Child's guide to the seven sacraments / by Elizabeth Ficocelli ; illustrations by Anne Catharine Blake.
        p. cm.
    ISBN 0-8091-6723-9 (alk. paper)
    1. Sacraments—Catholic Church—Juvenile literature. 2. Catholic Church—Doctrines—Juvenile literature. I. Blake, Anne Catharine. II. Title.

BX2200.F49 2005
264'.0208—dc22

2004029059

Published by Paulist Press
997 Macarthur Boulevard
Mahwah, New Jersey 07430

www.paulistpress.com

Printed and bound in Mexico

Dedicated with love
to Vince and Dorothy Ficocelli,
for their wonderful example
of sacramental marriage

E.F.

For Adam Jason Blake

A.C.B.

The Seven Sacraments

Baptism

Holy Communion

Reconciliation

Confirmation

Marriage

Holy Orders

Anointing of the Sick

Hi! My name is Dominic. I'm doing a report for school on the Seven Sacraments. *Sacraments* are words and actions that make God present to us in a special way. Jesus gave us sacraments so we can always feel his love for us. They also help us grow in faith to become good followers. Jesus loves us so much he gave us *seven* sacraments!

The first sacrament Jesus gave us is **Baptism.**

John the Baptist baptized Jesus in the Jordan River. Then Jesus went out and preached the Good News. Later, Jesus told his twelve special friends, the *apostles,* to *"go out and make disciples of all nations, baptizing them in the name of the Father, and of the Son, and of the Holy Spirit."*

I saw a baby get baptized in my church last week. The priest poured water over her head three times, baptizing her "in the name of the Father, and of the Son, and of the Holy Spirit." Just like Jesus said! Sometimes older children or even grown-ups may receive this sacrament if they haven't been baptized before.

In Baptism, our sins are washed away, and we become children of God and members of his Church. Baptism gives us a special gift, or *grace*, to believe in God, to love him, and to grow in goodness. Once we have been baptized, we have an important new job for the rest of our lives: to tell others about the love of Jesus.

Were you baptized? Ask a parent to tell you about it if you were too young to remember.

Even though our sins are washed clean in Baptism, as we grow older, we can still make choices that hurt others and separate us from God. That's why Jesus gave us another sacrament called **Reconciliation.** The word *reconciliation* means "to become friends again."

In the Bible, there are many stories about Jesus forgiving sins. After Jesus died and rose in glory, he appeared to his apostles. He breathed on them, sending them the power of the Holy Spirit. He also blessed them with the gift of bringing God's forgiveness to others. Jesus said, *"Receive the Holy Spirit. If you forgive anyone's sins, they are forgiven. But if you don't forgive their sins, they will not be forgiven."*

In the sacrament of Reconciliation, we receive the love and forgiveness of Jesus. Unlike Baptism, which only happens once, the sacrament of Reconciliation can be received again and again to help us stay close to Jesus.

Whenever I need to, I talk about my sins with my priest, Father Philip. This is called a *confession*. Father Philip helps me think of ways I can do better next time. He gives me a *penance*, something I can do to help make up for what I did wrong. Then he gives me God's forgiveness, or *absolution*. I feel much better, ready to start again!

What changes do *you* need to make to follow Jesus more closely?

The sacrament of Reconciliation helps me to be ready for another sacrament, **Holy Communion.** *Communion* means "to join together." Holy Communion is the most special and holy sacrament of all. Jesus gave us this sacrament because he loves us and wants to be with us always.

On the night before he died, at the *Last Supper*, Jesus blessed the bread he was about to share with his apostles and told them, *"Take this, all of you, and eat. This is my body given up for you."* Then he took the cup of wine and said, *"Take this, all of you, and drink. This is the blood of the new and everlasting covenant. Do this in memory of me."* At Mass, we do as Jesus asks by celebrating this holy meal, remembering his life and death, and receiving his Body and Blood.

Each time Father Philip offers the gifts of bread and wine at Mass, Jesus sends the Holy Spirit to change them into his Body and Blood. At this moment, Jesus becomes truly present to us in a special way we can't fully understand. This miracle lets Jesus feed all of his people, just like in the Bible story with the loaves and fishes. We praise God and thank him for such a great gift. Another word for thanks is *Eucharist*.

While food feeds my body, Holy Communion feeds my *soul.* It gives me the strength I need to follow Jesus more closely. Holy Communion joins all of us in a special way to Jesus, to his Church, and to each other. I'm happy to be fed by Jesus, so I receive this sacrament whenever I can!

At Mass, when bread and wine become Jesus' Body and Blood, how should we behave?

When I get older, I will receive another sacrament called **Confirmation.**
Once Jesus was baptized, God sent the Holy Spirit upon him in the form of
a dove. Then God said to Jesus, *"You are my own dear son, and I am pleased with
you."* This was Jesus' Confirmation.

After Jesus died and went to Heaven, he sent his apostles the Holy Spirit in the form of tongues of fire. This happened on a special day in the Church called *Pentecost*. By giving his apostles the gifts of the Holy Spirit, Jesus strengthened his friends with the power to preach about him and to perform wonders and miracles.

When we receive the Holy Spirit, it is *our* Confirmation.

My neighbor Julia was confirmed this year. It was a beautiful ceremony. The bishop came and blessed Julia and her classmates. He put oil on their foreheads, saying, *"Be sealed with the gift of the Holy Spirit."* To show that they are now "grown-up" followers of Jesus, each classmate chose a Confirmation name. This can be the name given to us at Baptism, or the name of a special saint. Julia chose the name Catherine.

Confirmation blesses us with all the gifts of the Holy Spirit. These gifts are wisdom, understanding, the ability to help and advise others, courage, knowledge, faithfulness, and respect for God. We need to pray to understand these gifts and to use them wisely. In Confirmation, we are like the apostles at Pentecost, called to be a light to the world and to share our love for Jesus.

Name one way you can be a light to the world.

Did you know there is one sacrament that takes *two* people to receive? It's the sacrament of **Marriage,** or *matrimony.*

Jesus has a special love for people who are married. He could have come into the world any way he wanted, but he chose to be born and raised in a family, *the Holy Family*—Jesus, Mary, and Joseph.

The first miracle Jesus performed in public was at a wedding in a town called Cana. This is another way Jesus lets us know how special and important marriage is to him.

Do you know what miracle this was? Read John 2:1–11 to find out.

My Mom and Dad have been married as long as I can remember. On their wedding day, they wore special clothes and promised God they would take care of each other for the rest of their lives. Father Philip gave them the blessing of the Church. They got lots of wedding gifts. Many times, God gives a married couple the best gift of all—children, like you and me!

When two people get married, they have to take care of each other and their children. But they also have another important job. Their love should show others how God loves his people and how Jesus loves his Church. The sacrament of Marriage helps the couple to be a good example, and it gives them strength when life is hard.

Not every grown-up gets married. Jesus calls people to serve him in different ways. Take Father Philip, for example. Father Philip was called to be a priest. He received the sacrament of **Holy Orders**.

Jesus is a priest, too. The king of priests! He taught his people, prayed with them, and healed them. Most of all, he served them, even giving his life for them. After Jesus gave his apostles the power of the Holy Spirit, he made them priests so they could continue building his Church on earth. The apostles chose more followers, laying their hands on them and sharing Jesus' priesthood.

Priests like Father Philip help to make Jesus present to us today as they serve God's people. When Father Philip celebrates Mass or a sacrament, he acts in the name of Jesus.

Of course, priests are not *really* Jesus; they are still human beings and can make mistakes just like you and me. But they try very hard to follow Jesus and to care for the people given to them. They choose not to get married and not to have children so they can give themselves more fully to God and his people.

What is the name of your priest? Can you think of one special job he does?

Sacraments help us all through our life. There's even one to help us when we are very sick or near death. It's called the **Anointing of the Sick.**

In the Bible, Jesus healed many people. He cured a blind man, a sick woman, and many lepers. He even raised people from the dead. These miracles helped people to believe in Jesus. The apostles were given this gift of healing, too. They shared this gift with others.

My best friend, Gregory, has a grandpa who is very sick and needs to have an operation. Father Philip visited him yesterday in the hospital. He blessed Gregory's grandpa with special oil and gave him the Anointing of the Sick. Sometimes this sacrament can make the person well. Sometimes it helps the person accept their suffering with love. If a person is dying, this sacrament can forgive sins and help that person be prepared for Heaven. I pray that Gregory's grandpa will get better!

Do you know someone who is very sick? Say a little prayer for that person now.

Look! I'm done with my report on the Seven Sacraments. Count them with me now: **Baptism, Reconciliation, Holy Communion, Confirmation, Marriage, Holy Orders,** and the **Anointing of the Sick**.

Each sacrament helps us to feel God's love and to grow stronger in our faith. I like to think of them as seven hugs from Jesus!

In what ways has Jesus hugged *you*?